Crab in a lab

Russell Punter

Illustrated by David Semple

At Sandy Cove, beside the sea,
lives little Sam the crab.

She likes to try experiments
inside her home-made lab.

The other crabs love teasing her.

"What use are brains?" they call.

"Who needs science?" cry the crabs.

Sam means to prove them wrong.

Inside her lab, Sam sets to work.

"I'll make a healthy drink.

If I mix some of this... with that...

Pew! What an eggy stink."

"I'll test this mixture next," gasps Sam.
She gives the flask a shake.

A flood of bubbles fills the lab.

Sam pours more mix into a tube
and rams the cork in tight.

But... CRASH! WHAM!

BANG!

Just then, she hears loud sounds outside.

She grabs some nearby coconuts
and fills them with her mix.

"Come and eat these nuts!" yells Sam.

The gannets swoop down fast.

But when they crack the nuts in two...

Starting to read

Even before children start to recognize words, they can learn about the pleasures of reading. Encouraging a love of stories and a joy in language is the best place to start.

About phonics

When children learn to read in school, they are often taught to recognize words through phonics. This teaches them to identify the sounds of letters that are then put together to make words. An important first step is for children to hear rhymes, which help them to listen out for the sounds in words.

You can find out more about phonics on the Usborne website at **usborne.com/Phonics**

Phonics Readers

These rhyming books provide the perfect combination of fun and phonics. They are lively and entertaining with great storylines and quirky illustrations. They have the added bonus of focusing on certain sounds so in this story your child will soon identify the *a* sound, as in **crab** and **lab.** Look out, too, for rhymes such as **fix – mix** and **fast – blast.**

Reading with your child

If your child is reading a story to you, don't rush to correct mistakes, but be ready to prompt or guide if needed. Above all, give plenty of praise and encouragement.

Edited by Lesley Sims
Designed by Hope Reynolds

Reading consultants: Alison Kelly and Anne Washtell

First published in 2023 by Usborne Publishing Limited, 83-85 Saffron Hill,
London EC1N 8RT, United Kingdom. usborne.com Copyright © 2023 Usborne Publishing Limited.
The name Usborne and the Balloon logo are registered trade marks of Usborne Publishing Limited.
First published in America 2023. UE